Bygone
FAREHAM

Publd. by Thos. Mansell, Fareham.

Engd. by Newman & Co. 48 Watling St. London.

View of Fareham, from Wallington Forts.

Bygone
FAREHAM

Pam Moore

Phillimore

1990

Published by
PHILLIMORE & CO. LTD.
Shopwyke Hall, Chichester, Sussex

ISBN 0 85033 736 4

Printed and bound in Great Britain by
BIDDLES LTD.
Guildford, Surrey

To the memory of my much loved grandfather,
George Sidney Lakin Smith (1891-1966),
who played such an important part in my childhood in Fareham.

List of Illustrations

Acknowledgements

All the pictures in this book are reproduced by the kind permission of the Hampshire County Museums service, with the following exceptions: Plates 34, 35, 79, 140, 141 Kay Ayland; Plates 36, 111 F. Bussey; Plates 56-58, 69, 70, 97, 102, 142, 144 Edwin Course; Plates 85, 86, 122, 145, 163 Roy Daysh; Plates 9, 33, 44, 60, 61, 63, 64, 71, 112, 166, 168 Phyl and Ken Jackson; Plates 50, 75, 76, 84, 95, 101, 155, 160 John Silman; Plates 3, 17, 19, 20, 46, 59, 67, 99, 125, 126, 151, 169 and the street plan, Bob Temple. I am grateful to them all. Plates 21, 22, 29, 37, 49, 62, 172 are from the author's collection.

I am most grateful to everyone who has helped in the production of this book. I am particularly indebted to those who have allowed me to use photographs, many of which have never before been published. I would like to thank Alastair Penfold, Curator of Fareham Museum, the staff of the Cope Collection, Portsmouth City Library; also the Department of Teaching Media, Southampton University. I am grateful to those who have assisted with information, especially Kay Ayland, Roy Daysh, Phyl and Ken Jackson and Bob Temple. Useful advice and comments on the book have been given by John Silman. To Edwin Course, I am grateful for advice, and for assistance in checking captions and commenting on the text. Above all, I would like to record my deep gratitude to my parents Phyl and Bob Spencer, for their help and support which has taken so many forms, including assistance in selection of photographs, obtaining information from Fareham residents, and for constant encouragement. Without them, this book would not have been produced.

Introduction

The history of Fareham, situated about ten miles west of Portsmouth in Hampshire, can be traced to Domesday and before, evidence of early settlement, including flints, having been found in some quantity. In the 1086 Survey, 'Fernham' was recorded as containing 30 hides, although it was only assessed at 20 because of the settlement's exposed position and liability to attack from the Danes.

By the medieval period Fareham was thriving, and its geographical location – on a creek leading from Portsmouth Harbour – influenced its fortunes. It was a free port, engaged in wine trading, and the building and repair of ships played an important part in the local industrial scene. For centuries, the Quay area of the town was to remain a focal point of economic life – indeed, it is, even today, integral to the townscape, although its character has changed considerably over the years.

So highly was Fareham regarded as a port and as a centre for the building and repair of ships that, in 1630, a letter was written to Sir John Coke, Principal Secretary of State, stating 'The river leading up to Fareham, within a mile of the town is an absolute good and safe place to moor ships, and in all respects as convenient and safe a harbour as Chatham'. Trade was also considerable and varied, with the movement of timber being important, and other exports including locally-produced bricks and pottery ware. Amongst imports, coal was of special importance.

The town also grew as a market centre, with an annual fair, and it was popular with retired and serving naval officers and their families. For centuries, the main thoroughfare of Fareham was its High Street, but in the Victorian period West Street gradually took over this role, and High Street, with its fine buildings, became less involved in the economic life of Fareham. In the present century, the town has spread in every direction, and the last 30 years have witnessed its transformation and dramatic growth in population.

This book concentrates almost entirely on the 19th and 20th centuries, and has been divided into 11 thematic sections. The port is one of these, and the illustrations of the Quay area show activity, vessels and buildings, spanning a period of almost 200 years. Arguably the most important area of the town historically, it receives wide coverage.

Other themes are also given attention, however. The book begins with a section on some local mansions, which looks at a selection of the more important houses in the town and its immediate surrounding area. As already mentioned, Fareham has for centuries attracted well-to-do people, especially of naval background – early 19th-century directories provide a fascinating glimpse into the composition of the population. The names of many admirals and captains can be found, a point noted by William Thackeray, who spent a great deal of his childhood in the town, staying with his grandmother. As well as the houses I have selected for inclusion, others survive, usually in re-use; for example, Uplands House, once home of the Jellicoe family, is now a retirement home.

Every town has churches and schools, many of which are closely linked to local history; Fareham is no exception. Its parish church has a long and complex story; other churches have interesting tales associated with them, too, including one with a highly inventive vicar (*see* plate 18)! As well as the provision of state education, which has developed mainly in the past century, Fareham had, for more than 250 years, a school bearing the name of one of the town's local worthies, William Price, founded under the generous terms of his will.

Fareham has a surprisingly rich industrial past; unfortunately many aspects of this have left little in the way of tangible remains. Fareham bricks and pottery were sent across the world, but the only evidence of this activity is in the products themselves – many of the town's buildings are constructed of local bricks, and quite a few of the distinctive 'Fareham chimney pots' survive. Fortunately, some illustrations of the local mills and the important tanyard are available, although the sites themselves have changed beyond recognition.

Although sea transport played such an important role in Fareham's story, the movement of people and goods by road and rail was also significant. It was fairly unusual for a town the size of Fareham to be served by electric trams, and the interest these aroused is reflected in the number of photographers who captured the system on film. Their work is an invaluable record.

Special times in Fareham's story, both happy and sad, seemed worthy of inclusion. Royal visits always provoke enthusiasm everywhere, and provide an opportunity for celebration. Although members of the royal family travelled through Fareham by train on occasion, the 'official' visit by Princess Beatrice in 1905 was long remembered in the town. A wide range of leisure pursuits have been followed in Fareham over the years, and these too have produced some interesting pictures of sporting and artistic achievement. Two World Wars left their mark on the people of Fareham, and this book would have been incomplete without reminders of those difficult times.

One of the most surprising facets of Fareham's history is the sheer spread of its development and growth this century, from a small market town and port, to an urban satellite, enjoying borough status and housing almost 100,000 people. The photographs of north Fareham – where Park Lane and Old Turnpike have completely changed in character in less than half a century – are reminders of how a tranquil rural area has been transformed into a busy urbanised area of high density building. As cars now roar on and off the motorway which has made Fareham so convenient for commuting to Portsmouth and Southampton, it is hard to imagine that just over a century ago horses and carts were the principal form of road transport, and that the need to pause at tollgates did not provoke major traffic jams.

The final section of the book, 'Street Scenes', illustrates graphically the changes which Fareham has undergone. These were, at first, gradual – conversion of some houses into shops, for instance. In the 1960s, where this book ends, the pace quickened. Fareham had long been a market centre; now the livestock market is no more. The wide main street has been pedestrianised, and many of the older buildings have been cleared to make way for a modern shopping mall. Today, redevelopment continues – as I write, sections of Portland Street are disappearing, and another part of Fareham is being transformed.

Having grown up in Fareham in the 1950s and '60s, I have been particularly aware of change – some of it for the better. However, Fareham has lost much of its heritage in the name of 'progress'; this book is intended to act as a reminder of change – both good and bad.

The Plates

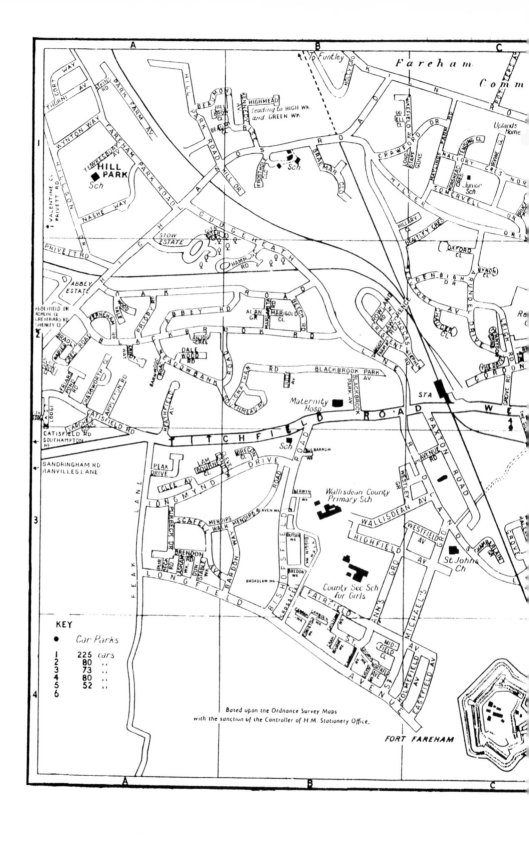

KEY

Car Parks

1	225	cars
2	80	,,
3	73	,,
4	80	,,
5		,,
6	52	,,

Based upon the Ordnance Survey Maps
with the sanction of the Controller of H.M. Stationery Office.

FORT FAREHAM

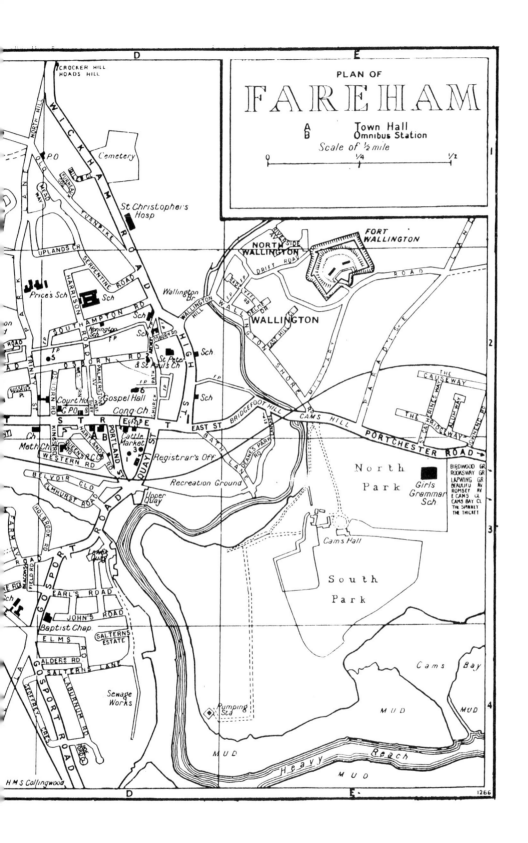

PLAN OF

FAREHAM

A   Town Hall
B   Omnibus Station

Scale of ½ mile

0   ¼   ½

Further Reading

The Buildings of England: Hampshire and the Isle of Wight, N. Pevsner and D. Lloyd, London 1967

Victoria County History of Hampshire, London 1908

The Story of Fareham, G. L. Privett, Winchester 1949

The Fareham of Yesteryear, Ron Brown, Horndean 1983

Fareham in Old Picture Postcards, John Emery, Zaltbommel 1985

The Industrial Heritage of Hampshire and the Isle of Wight, Pam Moore, Chichester 1988

Some Local Mansions

1. Westbury Manor, seen here in about 1920, is a fine building of mainly Georgian date, occupying a position in the heart of the town centre, in West Street. At the time of this photograph, it was still in use as a residence.

2. This glimpse of Westbury Manor, taken from across the street in the late 1930s, shows the building in the 'second phase' of its life, as the town's council offices. Following the construction of new civic offices in the 1970s, the Manor suffered a period of uncertainty, with its future in doubt. Now, after extensive renovation work, it will open in the early summer of 1990 as the Fareham Museum.

3. Close-up of Westbury Manor *c*.1945, during its period as council offices.

4. Cams Hall was once a house of considerable opulence, designed by Jacob Leroux in the late 18th century for the Delme family, who lived there for more than 100 years. Now the house is sad and derelict, facing an uncertain future. This view of the exterior dates from the year 1936, when it was still occupied.

5. The library at Cams Hall in 1936 – one of a set of photographs of the interior of the house now in the care of the Hampshire County Museums Service.

6. The nursery, Cams Hall, 1936. The rocking horse and the delightful frieze depicting Noah's Ark animals would surely prove a source of pleasure to any child.

7. 'Below stairs' – the kitchen at Cams Hall in 1936, with a traditional range, and cook taking a moment's break to pose for the photographer.

8.   Roche Court, on the road to Wickham, has its origins in the medieval period, with many later alterations and additions – Elizabethan, Georgian and Edwardian. It is now a private school.

9.   Outside Roche Court in the 1930s, the head gardener (on the left) Harry Sharp, and the gamekeeper Charlie Smith.

Fareham Churches

10.   The parish church of St Peter and St Paul as seen in this 1767 view, is mainly medieval, although the tower had been rebuilt in 1742. The base of the tower was of stone from the earlier structure, the remainder being in local brick.

11.   The church, *c.*1900, much changed from the previous view. In 1812 the nave was rebuilt and made larger, and towards the end of the 19th century Sir Arthur Blomfield was responsible for the erection of a new chancel. The medieval chancel was retained as a chapel.

12.   A photograph by Sidney Smith of St Peter and St Paul church in the 1930s, following additions in 1929 by Sir Charles Nicholson, who virtually rebuilt the nave of 1812. This view is taken from Osborne Road, looking east.

13. The Roman Catholic church, with its dedication to the Sacred Heart, stands just to the south of the town centre. Built in 1878, it is today little changed from this view of *c*.1930.

14. A view of part of West Street, c.1865, showing the 'Independent' chapel, later to be known as the Congregational and then the United Reformed church. The building dates from 1836, and its architect was probably Jacob Owen. Also in this view, the former Corn Exchange can be seen.

15. An Edwardian view of the Congregational church, with its gabled façade. This area is in the process of redevelopment; the church building will remain, but in adaptive re-use.

16. A Victorian engraving of West Street, showing Holy Trinity church. Of similar date – mid-1830s – to the Congregational church, it is likely both were the work of the same architect, Jacob Owen. Holy Trinity is built mainly of local brick, with its tower, erected shortly after the rest of the church, bearing a stone spire.

21. Sunday School pageant, Fareham Methodist church, 1961. The theme was 'England', with Britannia as the central figure (Mrs. June Ward). The author is kneeling in the centre of the picture.

22. The Methodist church had many links with the Temperance Movement and the 'Band of Hope'. In the early 1960s, members of the Junior Choir took part in 'Festivals of Queens', organised by the Band of Hope. This photograph of 1962 shows the 'Queen', Barbara Jones, with her attendants, (left to right) Patricia Day, Pam Spencer (author), Penny Ward and Brenda Coffin. The girls took part in events across southern England, as well as local functions, such as Portchester Carnival.

Fareham Schools

23. Price's School, which appears in later views, was founded in the 1720s with money bequeathed by William Price. It stood in West Street. In the early years of this century it was decided that the building was no longer suitable, and a new school was built. It is seen here on its opening day, in January 1908, with its 17 pupils.

24. A view of Price's School in the 1930s. The single-storey building on the left of the picture was the well-used school tuck shop. All the buildings shown here have now been demolished.

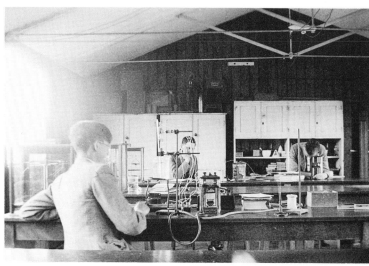

25. Science laboratory, Price's School, in the late 1930s.

26. Mr. S. R. Bradly, Headmaster of Price's from 1908 until 1934, pictured with his wife at the time of his retirement.

27. Price's Cadet Corps, shown in the summer of 1939. Three officers watch the boys pass, the one on the right being Mr. Hollingsworth.

28.   The Girls' Grammar School opened its doors in 1956, and was situated to the east of the town, near Cams Hall. It is now a mixed school – Cams Hill Comprehensive. This view of 1957 shows the 'official' opening. From left to right are the Headmistress, Miss M. E. Lowe, the Bishop of Portsmouth, and Miss R. Hillyard (now Mrs. Billett), who taught Art at the school.

29.   Playing fields of Fareham Girls' Grammar School, 1967. The three fifth formers are, from left to right, Sue Cowen, Pam Spencer (author) and Rosemary Sargent.

30. Class at Redlands Lane Junior School, *c*.1930. Note the universal fascination with the camera!

31.   Gordon Road Boys' School (now demolished) *c*.1930.

32.   The staff of Gordon Road Boys' School, pictured in the 1930s. Note the Headmaster's spats!

33. Gordon Road School football team, 1933. The Headmaster, Mr. Sims, is third from left in the back row; the Sports Master, Mr. Stone, is third from right. The identity of some of the boys is known – in the front row, Jimmy Wheeler is on the right, and next to him is Ken Jackson. Third from left in the front is Bert Collins, whose father was a butcher in Fareham.

34. The first intake to Harrison Road Girls' Secondary School, in 1934. Fourth from the left in the front row is Betty K. Daws (now Mrs. Ayland).

35.   Fareham Board School, Wickham Road, *c*.1907. Elsie Frost, mother of Betty Daws (see plate 34) is third from left in the top row. The Board School was built in 1877, with additions in 1894. It later became Fareham County Primary School, and is now an Adult Education Centre.

36. Fareham Board School, 1913. One wonders how many of these children lost fathers or brothers in the Great War which was soon to cast its shadow.

37. Mrs. Denise Barker with her class 3A, outside what had now become Fareham County Primary School in 1961. The author is in the centre of the front row.

38. Miss Jackson's class, Fareham Board School, *c*.1930. Miss Margaret Jackson taught at the school for more than 30 years.

39.   Staff of Fareham County Primary School in 1959. Back row (left to right): Mr. Walsh, Mrs. Williams, Mrs. Johnson, Mrs. Colebourne, Miss Poore, Mrs. Pinney, Mrs. Ryan, Mr. Nicholls. Front row (left to right): Mrs. Shepherd, Mr. Dimmer, Miss Jackson, Mr. Walker (Headmaster), Miss Ward, Mr. Hart, Mrs. Parsons.

40. Wykeham House School, High Street, *c*.1960. The building is of special interest. It is not, as it appears, constructed of yellow brick, but of red brick faced with mathematical tiles, added to suit a prevailing fashion in the 19th century.

41. Classroom in Wykeham House School, *c*.1930. The school remained in these premises until the mid-1980s – the building is now in office use.

Rural Fareham

42. Park Lane, to the north of the town centre, as it looked in the 1930s when local photographer Sidney Smith took this view. Many of the trees survive, but the appearance of rural idyll has gone – it is now a busy road, lined by modern houses.

43. North Hill, seen in the 1930s by Sidney Smith, looking towards the Wickham Road. Like Park Lane, it is now a busy thoroughfare, and houses not only line it, but have spread off to the west in a modern estate.

44. Old Turnpike, seen from its junction with North Hill and Park Lane. The post office shown in this view of *c*.1905 is now a private house; the public house, the *New Inn*, has been much altered and renamed the *Turnpike*.

45.   The Avenue runs west from Fareham towards Southampton. This 1930s' view gives an impression of its appearance before road widening and the building of houses took place right along its length.

46. A panoramic view of Wallington village and the river, *c.*1920. The bridge in the foreground survives, but is no longer used by vehicles.

47. The area close to the River Wallington has not suffered so much from development as the main town. This 1950s' postcard shows a stretch of the river bordered by meadows.

48. Another view of the river, with cottages backing on to it. These can still be seen, although there are now also a considerable number of modern dwellings in what is known as Wallington village.

The Industrial Past

49.   A view of Cams tide mill around the turn of the century. The sign on the building proclaims it to be the establishment of Mr. S. Harris – it is possible that he is the gentleman standing towards the right-hand side of the picture.

50.   A view of the back of the mill. The weatherboarded structure is already deteriorating and soon after the end of the First World War the decision was taken to demolish it. Today a plaque marks the spot where it stood.

51. The tannery at Wallington was, for many years, an important feature of the town's economic life. This view shows the interior of one of the buildings around the turn of the century.

52. Bark was essential for the tanning process, and this picture, *c.*1900, shows a cartload arriving at the works. Fareham Tannery closed down shortly before the First World War.

53. and 54.   Some of the former tannery buildings suffered a serious fire in the 1930s. These views show the damage clearly; the remainder of the works was demolished in the 1960s.

55.   An Edwardian advertisement for the Fareham Steam Laundry Co. Ltd. Their premises were situated on the Gosport Road; the buildings are very typical of their period.

Transport by Road and Rail

56. In the turnpike era, a number of tollgates could be seen around Fareham. This view shows that at the junction of Old Turnpike and Wickham Road (previously London Road), *c.*1880. On the right are the workhouse buildings of 1836, now St Christopher's Hospital. The tollhouse site is now occupied by a tyre company.

57. At the eastern end of the town travellers passed through the East Cams tollgate, seen here in about 1880, on their way to Portsmouth.

58. This view shows the tollgate on the road between Fareham and Southampton at the west end of the town. The photographer is standing at the crossroads, with Gudge Heath Lane on his left and Redlands Lane on his right, looking towards Fareham. Between the trees the railway bridge is just visible.

59. Looking towards Fareham from the west, *c*.1905. The photographer is standing east of the tollhouse, and the view is dominated by the railway arch, with a train running across it. The station is obscured by trees on the left of the picture.

60.   Fareham had an electric tram service linking it to Gosport from 1906 until 1929. This picture shows a tram, car No.4, at the terminus, just short of the railway station. The *West End Inn* has long since been demolished, but the houses on the left-hand side survive.

61.   This picture of *c.*1906 shows not only the tram, highlighting the lack of weather protection for the driver, but also, on the left-hand side, the old post office, when it was situated at the junction of West Street and Portland Street. This tram is travelling from Gosport to Fareham and has just turned the corner into West Street, on its way to the terminus.

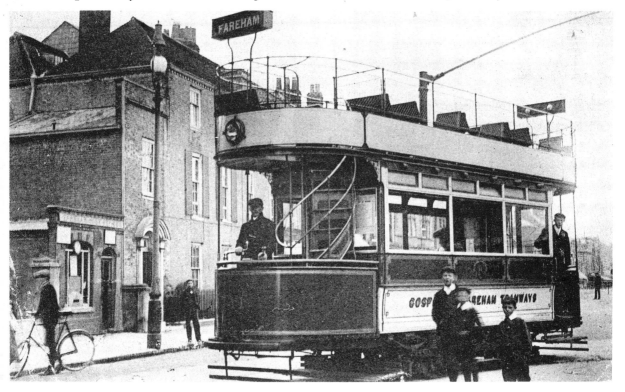

62.   In this Edwardian view, tram car No. 5 has left the terminus and is heading east along West Street. It is just passing Holy Trinity church and the junction of West Street and Trinity Street.

63. A postcard view of a tram in a similar position to that in plate 61, but showing more of the town. The former Corn Exchange is the white building on the corner of Portland Street. It is now Portland Chambers, and little changed externally.

64. This scene would be quite unrecognisable today. It shows the road to Gosport; the cottages have disappeared and their site is now covered by a roundabout and flyover. Of the trams, a solitary traction pole by the *Bird in Hand* public house on the way into Fareham is the only above ground reminder, although much of the track survives, buried beneath the road surface.

65. The name Fred Dyke was synonymous with transport in Fareham for many years. This view shows one of his horse-drawn vehicles, on this occasion on its way to appear at the Fareham and Hants Farmers' Show, held at Roche Court on 29 August 1934.

66. A fascinating photograph taken in the early years of the century, showing some of Fred Dyke's vehicles parked by Fareham viaduct. Fred Dyke's haulage business thrived in Fareham for many years; his wife was very active, too, in local civic and charitable affairs (see later plates).

67. Fareham bus station, *c*.1945. This view captures the atmosphere of the immediate post-war period. Some buses retain white painted mudguards; an examination of the people reveals a number of service personnel in uniform.

68.   The railway station, part of which was designed by Sir William Tite, was opened in 1841. This engraving shows the station approach in the 1850s.

69.   F. G. O. Stuart, the Edwardian photographer, captured the same view about 50 years later, with remarkably little change. Wheeled transport still depends on the horse, and an air of tranquillity prevails. Some additions had been made to the station in 1889, but Tite's building can still be seen.

70. A closer view of the railway station in the early years of this century. If taxis were substituted for the carriages, the scene would be little altered today.

71. The bridge which carried vehicular traffic across Fareham Creek, shown around the turn of the century. The houses in the background are those which stretched along Wallington Shore Road.

72.   The bay platform of Fareham station in the early 1950s, showing a train about to leave for Alton. This travelled over the Meon Valley line, which opened in 1903 and closed to passengers in 1955.

73.   A train passing Fareham East signal box (now demolished), coming into the station from Alton.

74.   The alterations being made to Fareham tunnel *c.*1906, following the decision to make the track single at this point and use it for Meon Valley trains only.

75. and 76.   These two views both show the impressive 17-arch brick viaduct of 1848, which carried the railway across Fareham Creek. Both by F. G. O. Stuart, the view above is taken from the Fareham side, looking towards Cams Mill and the road to Portchester. The date is around 1900. A steamroller pulling a mess hut for the use of workmen engaged in road maintenance can be seen. The picture below shows the scene looking towards the viaduct from the bottom of East Street.

Fareham and War

77. The war memorial at Fareham being unveiled on 2 July 1921. The ceremony was performed by Earl Haig, and the military guard and local clergy can be seen in this view. The memorial, of stone from the Forest of Dean, can still be seen in front of Holy Trinity church.

78. Remembrance Day, November 1956. Major Sutton, the local British Legion president, salutes the war memorial.

79. Fareham fire brigade in 1940, preparing to leave the town to relieve the London station. Alderman Tommy Keen is wishing them well (centre); Betty Daws holds a horseshoe on the left-hand side of the picture – many generations of her family served with the fire brigade.

80.   A tractor pulls a plough along West Street with the slogan 'Plough for Victory', during the Second World War. It has just passed Savoy Buildings – the photographer is standing near the top of Hartlands Road.

81.   Land Army girls in cheerful mood at Fareham in about 1940.

82.   Issue of ration books in Fareham, 1940.

83.   The end is in sight! A happy group from Birdwood Grove on V.E. Day, May 1945.

Special Occasions

84.   On Wednesday 4 October 1905, Queen Victoria's youngest daughter, Princess Beatrice (by this time Princess Henry of Battenburg), visited Fareham with her daughter Princess Ena (later Queen of Spain). This was indeed an exciting day for the town, and this view shows people waiting at the railway station for a glimpse of the royal visitors.

85.   (*opposite above*) This picture shows the Princess's procession moving along West Street, with an escort of mounted police, and crowds lining the route which had been decorated with bunting and evergreen. The Princess had come to open a bazaar in aid of funds to improve Holy Trinity church (the rebuilding of the chancel).

86.   (*opposite below*) The Princess acknowledges the cheering crowds. The bazaar was held in the Connaught Drill Hall and, after being greeted by local dignitaries, Princess Beatrice and her daughter were presented with bouquets of flowers. The Princess declared the bazaar 'open' and toured the many stalls and sideshows, before leaving Fareham in the car of Mr. Arthur Lee, the local M.P.

PRINCESS HENRY OF BATTENBURG AT FAREHAM. OCT 4TH 08
CHILDREN SINGING

87.   The South Hants election
declaration in 1910, showing the
victorious candidate, Arthur Lee, and his
wife. Mr. Lee had been Conservative
M.P. for South Hampshire Division for 10
years. Later, as Lord Lee of Fareham, he
was to present 'Chequers' to the nation
for the use of future Prime Ministers as
their country retreat.

88. and 89.   These views show the emergency feeding demonstration which took place at Westbury Manor on 4 March 1954. In the picture above are (left to right) Mrs. E. Fritchley (W.V.S. Head of the Welfare Section of the Civil Defence, Fareham), Cllr. Riley (Chairman of F.U.D.C.), Mrs. M. Albrow (W.V.S. Emergency Feeding Officer), Mrs. E. Tatford, Mrs. H. Bishop and Mrs. Dyke (W.V.S. Centre Organiser for Fareham) with Mrs. Horner crouching in front. The photograph below shows Cllr. Riley and Mrs. Fritchley inspecting another part of the demonstration.

90.   Welfare foods meeting, 1955; Mrs. Dyke and Mrs. Fitchley can again be seen.

91.   A funeral cortège passing the workhouse en route to Fareham cemetery on 20 February 1909. The deceased was Mr. Edgar Goble, who died suddenly at a fire brigade dinner. Mr. Goble was a well-respected Fareham figure – a solicitor, the local coroner, and the Hon. Secretary of the Industrial Home for Girls at Wallington, later St Edith's Children's Home, and now the *Roundabout Hotel*.

92. In 1948 the old workhouse became St Christopher's Hospital. This photograph shows the chef with Matron, preparing for Christmas in the late 1950s.

93. Nurses at St Christopher's decorating a ward to bring Christmas cheer to their patients.

Maritime Fareham

94. An early painting, titled 'The Port of Fareham', this views the scene from Lower Quay looking across in the direction of the town. Although it appears idyllic, the port was, at this time, still busy with commercial traffic.

95. This postcard shows the same view around 1905. The railway viaduct of 1848 now divides the town centre from the Quay area. Otherwise the scene has changed little.

96. A view of the Quay at low tide *c.*1920. The part of the Quay near the viaduct is deserted in this scene, but has in fact retained a little commercial traffic even today, when the rest of the area is devoted to pleasure craft.

97. Looking from under the viaduct towards Lower Quay, this postcard of *c.*1925 shows the traction poles for the electric trams and, in the background, the steam flour mill and other industrial buildings. The drinking fountain in the foreground was given to the town by Mr. Thomas Burrell, whose family were local coal and corn merchants.

98. A view of Lower Quay *c*.1930. On the left is a warehouse of 1912 and, partially obscured by a vessel, the steam flour mill is just visible. Fred Dyke's premises, housed in the former electricity generating station, are next door.

99. Fareham Lower Quay, 1946. This close view of the buildings adjacent to the steam flour mill shows the way in which the quay kept its atmosphere until relatively recently. The Fareham chimney pots with their distinctive white bands are particularly noticeable in this photograph.

THE QUAY, FAREHAM

SIDNEY SMITH
PHOTOGRAPHER

26

100.   A coal-carrying vessel, the *Ngamdna*, dominates this scene, with three other craft visible. A group of children are bathing in this 1930s' view, although the purity of the water must have been somewhat doubtful. In the Victorian period, Fareham was a sea bathing resort for a time, but discarded German submarines following World War One led to pollution by the 1920s.

101. A twilight view of one end of Lower Quay *c.*1908. The large warehouse (see plate 98) has not, of course, been built, but the steam flour mill can be seen on the right of the picture.

102. A locally-produced card of about 1900, featuring several craft, including a sailing barge carrying sand.

103. An unusual view of the Quay area, taken from the recreation ground for a 1950s' postcard.

104. A picture of Fareham Regatta which, in the Victorian period, was one of the highlights of the town's year. This painting of *c*.1870 shows the spectators watching craft taking part, with the viaduct in the background.

105.   Fareham's steam flour mill opened in about 1830 and traded for well over 100 years. This photograph shows the staff at the time of closure in 1960. The building was used for light industry for some years; recently it has been converted for residential use.

Fareham at Leisure

106.   Fareham carnival, 1949. The Townswomen's Guild float.

107.   Townswomen's Guild performance of 'Hiawatha' in 1954.

108. Gosport and Fareham beagle pack, seen in the grounds of Fareham Park, 1909.

109. Boxing Day hunt meet outside the railway station, 1937.

110.   Art exhibition in the Assembly Hall, 1 June 1953.

111.   Fareham football club after cup success in 1931. The team includes Mr. F. Bussey, a local butcher.

112.   Fareham football club, 1946-7 season. Amongst the team are Sidney Saywell (third from left, back row), Ken Jackson (second from right, back row), Maurice Landport (right, back row), and, with the cup, Percy Lawrence (son of the proprietor of the *Royal Oak*).

Fareham at Work

113.   The *Red Lion Hotel, c.*1930. This building has a rich history. A well-known coaching inn, it is mentioned in William Cobbett's writings. It was also a posting house and excise office and, early in the 20th century, the 'Harmony' Lodge of Freemasons met here. Note the A.A. sign on the right-hand side of the hotel; like most of its kind, this has long since been removed.

114. The *Royal Oak*, on the corner of Trinity Street, opposite Holy Trinity church. This public house survives, although it has undergone changes – both in name and appearance.

115. Pyle's *Temperance Hotel* stood on the opposite corner of Trinity Street to the *Royal Oak*, at 161 West Street. The Pyle family, who were Methodists, owned a number of premises in Fareham, including a long-established bakery at 31 West Street. Southern Gas showrooms now occupy the site of the *Temperance Hotel*.

116. The Cedar Cottage tea rooms were situated in East Street, at the top of Bath Lane. This photograph, taken in the 1920s by Sidney Smith, shows the site a few years before it was transformed into a petrol station (see plate 165).

117. This view of A. W. Clark's establishment, c.1910, shows the staff posed formally in front of their Portland Street premises, which sold beers, wines and spirits.

118. W. G. Abraham's shop, near the bottom of High Street, was a very long-established business – about 100 years – when this photograph was taken in the 1920s. It proclaims its trade as 'Upholsterer and Cabinet Maker', but also sold china, glass and furniture, operated an undertaker's business, and acted as wine merchants.

119. and 120. The premises of Willcox, builders, were situated in High Street. For many years, until *c.*1910, the business was run in the names of C. & A. Blackman. The advertisement is typical of the Edwardian period, and comes from a town guide.

41

121. Egbert Neville was in business in Fareham as a chemist by the early years of this century. The shop interior is typical of an Edwardian pharmacy.

122. This view of *c*.1905 shows the premises of Darby's, electrical, sanitary, gas and hot water engineers, situated on the corner of Quay Street, opposite the *Bugle Hotel*. The shop's ownership changed many times, but it remained a hardware business as Radford's and G. A. Day Ltd.

123. and 124.   Two 1918 advertisements from a local newspaper.

125. Premises of W. H. Jeffery in Trinity Street, *c*.1920. The proprietor is standing outside. The Jefferys were well-known furnishers in the town for many years.

126. M. Taylor and Son was a traditional grocery shop, as can be seen in this view of *c*.1905 with Mr. Taylor in the doorway. Their advertisements proclaimed them as 'Cheese Factors and Provisions Merchants'.

E. J. HINXMAN

FAREHAM MOTOR & CARRIAGE WORKS

MOTOR REPAIRS.—Complete Overhauls undertaken. Painting and Upholstering executed by competent workmen on the premises.

Sole Agent for Fareham. "Cyclean" process for decarbonising Cars without dismantling.

Complete Stock of Accessories.
Michelin Tyres Stockist.
Accumulators charged.   Petrol.

HIGH STREET BRANCH :

CYCLES from **£3 : 10 : 0** complete.

ACCESSORIES at Lowest Prices combined with Best Quality.

Sole Agent for "**Marathon**" Gramophones and Records.

Record twice as long as those of average make at the same price.

"**Empire**" Records, 1/6 each, double-sided.

Call and hear them.   Inspection invited.

Illustration from photo, taken on customer.

Tel. 36x

RIDING and MOTOR OUTFITS for Gentlemen.
Absolutely correct in style and of dependable materials.

BREECHES for Riding, Shooting, Golf, and every description of Sport, from **21/-**

RIDING, SHOOTING, & SPORTING SUITS in Tweeds and Homespuns, from **60/-**

CHAUFFEUR'S LIVERY, Coat, Breeches and Cap   from **50/-** inclusive

MOTOR OVERCOATS   from **45/-**

L. TRIGG, Tailor & Outfitter,
WEST STREET, FAREHAM

127-136.   These advertisements all appeared in a local newspaper in 1918.

137. Fareham continued to have a livestock market until the 1960s. This photograph shows Stuart Wyatt, the market's certifying officer, with the grading officer of the day, engaged in the grading of sheep in the mid-1950s.

138. This Hereford steer was judged best in its class at the Christmas fatstock show of 1959, and fetched a record price for cattle sold at auction in Fareham market.

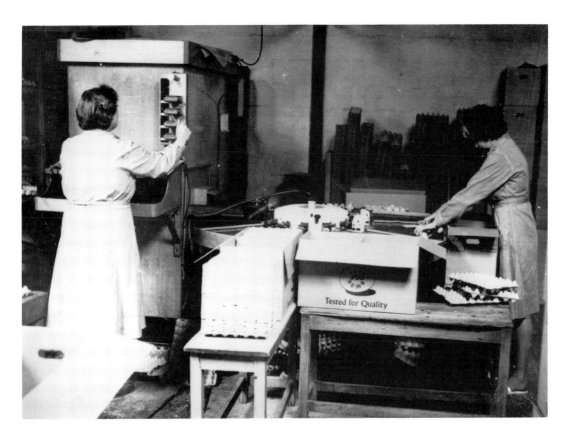

139. Market employees in the 1950s, grading and packing eggs. The eggs were fed on to a moving belt at one end of the machine and passed through a vertical enclosed compartment where lights revealed cracked or bad specimens. The eggs then moved to the revolving table on the right, and were graded by weight and size.

140. Fireman John Frost, caretaker of Fareham fire station, c.1910. Several generations of the Frost family served in Fareham's fire brigade.

141. Fareham fire brigade shown in the early 1920s outside the fire station with a very early petrol-driven engine.

Street Scenes

WEST STREET, FAREHAM.

142.   A view of the west end of West Street, showing the spire of Holy Trinity church. Taken in about 1920, the traction poles and track for the electric tram are in evidence. Otherwise, it is noteworthy that most of this part of Fareham is still residential.

143. A similar viewpoint, photographed about 10 years later. The trams have gone, and already change is taking place. The 'Regent' petrol station hints at the growing importance of the motor car. Shops have replaced residences in this area – today it is almost unrecognisable.

144. West Street at its junction with Osborne Road in about 1906. The little boy on the right stands beneath a lamp which indicates the way to the police station.

GENERAL POST OFFICE FAREHAM.

145. The post office, *c.*1907, soon after its opening on the site at the top of Hartlands Road. The horse-drawn vehicles are typical of the period.

146. A later view of the post office and the junction of West Street with Hartlands Road, taken in the 1920s
– the tram track and traction poles are still evident.

147. A decade later in Sidney Smith's photograph of the same scene the trams have disappeared, and more dwellings have
been replaced by shops. A telephone kiosk has now been installed in front of the post office.

148.   West Street in the 1930s. This part of the town remained relatively unaltered until the major changes of the 1960s. It has now been transformed.

149.   Moving east from the post office, this view of about 1930 shows the Alexandra cinema (to be replaced within a few years by the Embassy, with MacDonalds on the site today), and beyond it the street lined by residences up to the junction with Portland Street. On the right, the front garden of Westbury Manor can be glimpsed.

150.   Another Sidney Smith photograph, showing the transformation which occurred in the 1930s. The thick trees and residences on the left-hand side of the photograph above have been replaced by Savoy Buildings – a parade of shops and a new cinema. The shops survive, although much altered; F. W. Woolworth's store now occupies the Savoy cinema site.

151. A view of West Street, c.1945. Both the Embassy and Savoy cinemas are visible on the right of the picture; on the left is the entrance to the bus station, and the front of the Wesleyan chapel, by this time disused.

152. Thackeray House was owned by the novelist's grandmother, and stood on the corner of Portland Street. Thackeray spent much of his childhood there, and described Fareham as a 'dear little town'. The house later became a library and reading room, and was demolished in the 1930s to make way for a bus station.

153. A view of about 1910 of the West Street/Portland Street junction. The former Corn Exchange, Thackeray House and the Wesleyan chapel of 1875 can be seen on the right-hand side.

154. The eastern end of West Street in 1836 – note the survival of houses in the centre of the thoroughfare.

155. The same view about 80 years later – the houses have disappeared, giving a wide road. On the right are the Congregational church and the former Corn Exchange which had, by this time, become the town hall.

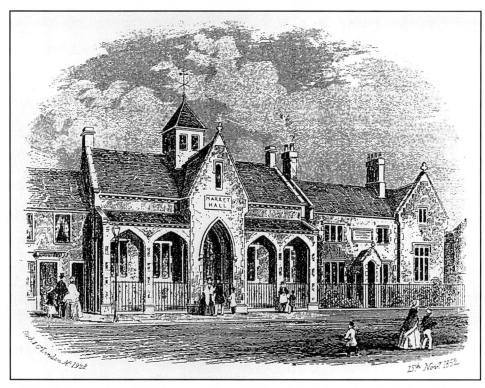

156. This engraving of 1852 shows the Market Hall, built in 1842, and the first Price's School, on the south side of West Street between Portland Street and Quay Street. The schoolmaster at this time was a Mr. Daniel Wrapson, who was also hall-keeper.

157. A photograph taken in the early years of this century of the same view. Price's School has been demolished and replaced by the town fire station – its engine stands outside.

158.   The eastern end of West Street looking west, pictured in the 1930s. Cars are now being parked where a century before houses had stood; a petrol station is in evidence at the left-hand edge of the picture.

159.   The same view in the 1950s shows clearly the dramatic increase in traffic which had taken place. Today this area is only pounded by feet, having been pedestrianised a decade ago.

160. West Street, showing its junction with High Street and East Street, in about 1905. Although most of the buildings on the left-hand side have survived, they have been much altered, with names like Suttons the booksellers now part of Fareham history.

FINE ART CALENDARS, ALMANACKS and DIARIES, At SUTTON'S LIBRARY.

161. The same scene about 20 years later. Only the tailor's shop continues the same trade today, though under another name.

162. A 1950s' view of the eastern end of West Street. Tom Parker's horse-drawn milk floats remained a feature of the town until the 1960s.

163.   Looking down Portland Street towards the railway viaduct and quay, this view of 1906 shows the new trams, and Clark's Wine Merchants on the left. Today, many of these buildings are being swept away as redevelopment takes place.

164.   A rare view of Union Street *c*.1930. The street was so named because prior to 1836 the workhouse was situated here. The corner of the *Red Lion Hotel* can be glimpsed in the background.

36. EAST STREET. FAREHAM.

SIDNEY SMITH
Photographer.

165.   A tranquil moment in East Street, recorded in the 1930s, and showing the then fairly new Cedar Garage. This establishment was demolished a few years ago and the site used for housing.

166. High Street, at its junction with West Street, shown *c*.1900. Next to Abraham's, Fareham Cycle Works now offers service for motor vehicles. Although the blinds fronting these shops have gone, the holes for their support are still visible in the pavement.

167. About 30 years have passed, but the scene has not greatly changed, save for the ownership of the shops and the evidence of motor vehicles. Although cycles are still catered for, it is noticeable that the car is becoming more important.

168. A view of High Street, *c.*1905, still tranquil and untroubled by motor vehicles. Although many aspects of Fareham would have changed by the time the baby in the perambulator had grown up, this part of the town, designated a conservation area, has remained relatively unspoiled, with its fine Georgian buildings.

169.   High Street *c*.1960, looking south. This picture shows clearly the fine Victorian lamp standards which survive today, and demonstrates the street's width – a reminder that it once housed the town's market.

170. Paxton Road, a residential street at the west end of Fareham, shown *c.*1930. The post office on the corner was run by Mr. L. Jeffery.

171. A view of Church Path in 1932, looking north. These attractive cottages survive, little changed since they were built in the 1890s, in an area otherwise unrecognisable.

172.   Palmerston Avenue, a quiet cul-de-sac to the north of West Street, shown in the 1950s. It survives, itself little altered, but surrounded by a brick and concrete jungle of the shopping centre and multi-storey car park.